Responsibility in the Classroom

A Teacher's Guide to Understanding and Motivating Students

Amy Lew, Ph.D. and Betty Lou Bettner, Ph.D.

Connexions Press

Acknowledgment

The authors are indebted to Alfred Adler and Rudolf Dreikurs for developing the techniques that provide the inspiration for their work.

3rd printing: 2008

ISBN-10: 0-9624841-0-5
ISBN-13: 978-0-9624841-0-0

Connexions Press
10 Langley Road, Ste. 200
Newton Centre, MA 02459
tel.: 617-332-3220
fax: 617-332-7863
e-mail: connexpr@thecia.net

and

Connexions Press
1 Old State Road
Media, PA 19063
tel.: 610-566-1004
fax: 610-566-1004
e-mail: blbettner@aol.com

website: www.connexionspress.com

CONTENTS

Society at Risk

No one needs to tell teachers that our society and our children are at risk, or that teachers themselves are at risk. Teachers encounter and cope with that reality every day.

There was a time when the distinction between the jobs of parents and teachers was clearer and more definite than it is today. Today, many of the tasks of parenting fall more heavily on teachers than they did in the past. This shift is one of the major consequences of the increase in parents' working outside the home, the rise of the single-parent family, and the growing percentage of children born into poverty. These forces combine with the fast-paced and over-packed nature of present day life to make it more likely that children will receive less and less parenting at home and that teachers will be spending more time making up the deficit with less time for academic teaching. Unfortunately most teacher education programs put most of their emphasis on how to teach the subject matter and provide little if any training in how to deal with classroom situations that interfere with learning. Without enough courses in understanding human behavior and group dynamics, teachers are left with few strategies and little confidence in their ability to confront this new educational requirement.

A paper entitled "Protecting Adolescents from Harm" published in the *Journal of the American Medical Association* (vol. 278, no.10, September 10, 1997, pp. 823 ff.) presented findings from the National Longitudinal Study on Adolescent Health. Based on interviews with over 12,000 adolescents in grades 7 through 12, the study identified risk and protective factors in the areas of emotional health, violence, substance use (alcohol, cigarettes, marijuana), and sexuality. The researchers looked at the family, the school, and the individual and found that parent-family connectedness and the perceived connectedness of school with young people were protective against every risk studied with the exception of pregnancy. (Concerning pregnancy, the study found that parental disapproval of early sexual activity was associated with delay of intercourse.)

Children everywhere want love and connection, want to feel valued and respected, and want to belong to family and community, whether at home, on the playground, or in school. Yet financial and emotional scarcity often create situations in which this nurturing and developmental encouragement are hard to come by. It often results in children learning to compete instead of cooperate, demand instead of negotiate, take instead of give and take. When these forces take hold, the home and the classroom begin to seem as unstable as a house of cards, with each added stress threatening to bring down the whole structure.

Not surprisingly then, there is a lot of concern about the future. Parents and teachers worry about the high incidence of teenage drug and alcohol abuse, teen gangs and violence, crime and suicide, and the general alienation of our youth. They also worry about the growing number of divorces and teen parents and the "me first" attitude of many of our young people.

These grim trends cause all of us serious concern. But as marriage and family therapists who are actively involved in parent and teacher education, and as parents ourselves, we are optimistic. We believe that teachers can still manage to be good teachers and have professionally fulfilling lives, and that children can still accomplish their major developmental tasks and become productive, happy adults in satisfying relationships. This book is about how teachers can take a major role in helping to carry out this process successfully – and can do so without short-changing the academic teaching to which they are committed.

The adult-child relationship we advocate does not tell parents and teachers to lay down the law, make stricter rules, and demand obedience. As any teacher knows, it's a lot easier to *make* the rules than to *enforce* them. When adults try to make children behave, the kids escalate their defiance or withdraw and hide what they are doing. Whatever positive relationship there may have been is eroded by the adults' becoming distrustful law enforcers, and whatever respect the children may have had for the adults is eroded by their laying down laws they can't enforce. If law enforcement isn't the answer, then what do children need and what can parents and teachers do? Let's go back to the beginning to look at what children need and what can happen if they don't get it.

Giving children what they need

Several years ago some research was undertaken to discover why some children become successful and others do not. The findings, which are entirely consistent with those of the National Longitudinal Study, are very clear regarding those differences—children who succeed have close relationships to others, feel valued in their communities, and have a sense of control over some aspects of their lives; children who are in trouble feel isolated, useless to society, and powerless.

The kids in trouble are missing four necessities that each child must have in order to successfully meet life's challenges. These necessities are not rules, not something children have to master and consciously remember. They are beliefs that teachers, parents and other adults can foster in children that will serve as unconscious behavioral guides. These beliefs are the internal certainty of—

- Being **connected** to others, a part of family, school, and community,
- Having the **capability** to take care of oneself,
- Being valued by others, the knowledge that one **counts** and makes a difference, and
- Having **courage**.

We call these four vital protections—**connection, capability, counting,** and **courage**—the **Crucial Cs** because they are the foundation for raising and teaching kids who can meet the challenges of these difficult times and become—

- Responsible
- Productive
- Cooperative
- Self-reliant
- Resilient
- Resourceful
- Contributing
- Happy
- And not incidentally, better learners

We'll look first at how these vital attributes help to protect children in childhood and enable them to become adults capable of contributing to family and society. We'll look at what parents and teachers can do to impart this internal protection to children and foster the growth of their capacities to lead rewarding adult lives. We will also give teachers a guide for understanding why children behave as they do and some suggestions on how teachers can promote students' acquisition of the Crucial Cs in the classroom.

The approach we recommend not only helps children meet developmental goals; it helps parents and teachers to lead lives of achievement and fulfillment, as well. What we present here is a blueprint for teachers to conduct classroom life that is beneficial to both teachers and children.

Four Vital Protections: The Crucial Cs

The enduring need to be connected

Human beings are social animals. Since we have no shell, no claws, no fangs, and no wings and since we are not stronger or faster than our enemies, we have had to band together for survival. We need to experience this connection for both physical and psychological security. Our survival depends on our ability to connect with others. This theme of dependence on connection with others takes different forms at different stages of life, but it runs throughout our lives. Developmentally, the most important task is to move from being totally dependent on others to being interdependent with others. This is not only for our own survival but to ensure the survival of the species. Therefore, necessity dictates that as soon as possible members of the social group make contributions to the group as well as take benefits from it. The nature of our connection then shifts from being dependent on others to becoming someone upon whom others can depend.

Infancy. The human infant's first need is to be connected, and if this first need is not met, the child will die. We cannot lift our heads at birth, much less crawl about in search of food. And our dependence on being connected to another is by no means limited to mealtimes. We are dependent on others for protection, shelter, and training in the skills we will need to take care of ourselves. This process of moving from dependence to independence takes a relatively long time.

Beyond the basic physical needs, the baby has emotional needs as well, and these, too, are met only in relationships. Bonding with the caregiver is the first way in which these needs are met. Nature serves the infant especially well here because bonding is also the caregiver's earliest emotional reward for performing the demanding task of providing for the newborn.

When an infant's needs to be held, caressed, and talked to are not met, the infant's capacity to relate to others will not develop. In time the child may withdraw into a state of remoteness in which he or she may not be *able* to connect with others. When all of these needs are met from the beginning, however, the baby will thrive and develop to full potential.

The job of the primary caregiver through this first connection is to ensure the survival of the infant while it is totally dependent and to foster the opportunities for the child to gain the capacity for greater independence and later interdependence.

Childhood. As infants grow they begin to develop their capabilities and move from total dependence towards a greater capacity for independence. Children must, however, develop new ways to connect to others so that they can take their place in society. Childhood is the time to actively experiment with different ways of relating and to try out various forms and degrees of both independence and interdependence. Through this process of trial and error, the child arrives at a set of beliefs about the world and what is possible, a strategy for living, and a set of behaviors to carry out the strategy.

Children who develop positive feelings of connection with their families have the confidence they need to reach out to others, make friends, and cooperate. When they are grown, they are more likely to develop mutually supportive, intimate relationships.

Children who are unsure of their ability to connect with others may feel insecure, isolated, and scared. They will do whatever they think they have to do to find a place. This may mean being the "perfect" child, the "bad" child, the clown, the scapegoat, or any number of other roles. They may seek attention to prove they have a place. The main point is that each of us develops an idea about what we must do in order to connect to those we depend upon.

Even in a family where the child is neglected or abused, the child must find someone with whom to connect in order to survive and to achieve psychological security. A child in a dysfunctional family does not realize that his or her family is different from others. Some children will connect with an abuser who appears to have the power; others will ally themselves with a parent who doesn't protect them but shows concern.

Adolescence. As children enter adolescence and their teen years, we can clearly see the effects of their beliefs about belonging and connection. Young people who are confident about their place in the group are able to participate and cooperate. They can be leaders or followers depending on the needs of the situation. These teens are able to decide when to go along with the crowd and when to say no because they are not afraid that they will be rejected or isolated. Youth who do not feel secure about their ability to connect are more susceptible to peer pressure. They believe that they must go along with the crowd or be ostracized.

Does the child CONNECT in a constructive way?

The child who does not connect in a constructive way—	The child who connects in a constructive way—
• Feels **insecure**	• Feels **secure**
• Feels isolated	• Can reach out
• Is more susceptible to peer pressure	• Can make friends
• Seeks **attention**	• Can **cooperate**
• May conclude that connecting in a negative way is better than not connecting at all	

If the child believes that he or she can connect in a positive way, the child does connect constructively.

Children who connect in a constructive way can say with conviction, "I believe that I belong."

The need to develop competence and feel capable

If people are to move along the road from dependence to interdependence they must also develop the ability to be independent. When we refer to "independence" in human beings, we mean some degree of self-sufficiency in performing certain tasks. The developing child's achievements in the direction of independence and the increasing capacity to take care of oneself are the foundation of the belief in oneself as competent and capable.

Infancy. Infants, who begin life able only to cry, squirm, and suck, gradually learn to hold up their heads, roll over, stand, and walk. No one has to force them to try; they do it for the pure joy of it. We only have to watch a young child learning to walk to realize that this drive to develop toward independence is innate. Nobody else could reward us enough to get us to fall down as often as we do while learning to walk; and yet, as children, we try over and over and each step brings with it the reward of accomplishment usually evidenced by an enormous grin!

Childhood. As children grow they must be given opportunities to develop their competence through real jobs and activities. Parents who are often stressed and in a hurry may find it easier to do things themselves, but this mistake may have dire consequences. Children may interpret parents' failure to assign them meaningful work as a vote of no confidence in their ability to do things themselves. They also may compare themselves to adults and older siblings who seem to be able to do everything and decide that since they are not as capable as others, they shouldn't even bother to try. If they decide that others are trying to keep them dependent, they may feel resentful or inadequate. Worse, they may comfortably settle into the role of pampered child with no responsibilities.

These children may become overly dependent on others or may allow others to treat them disrespectfully because they are afraid to be on their own. They may interpret others' behavior as controlling whether it is or not. They may become so confused that they believe that control is a sign of competence and independence. Moreover, they may become so impressed with the idea of control that they will try to show their own power by bossing others or proving that others can't tell them what to do. They may respond to even an ordinary request as if it were an unreasonable demand.

Does the child believe himself or herself to be CAPABLE?

The child who does not believe in his or her capability—	The child who believes in his or her capability—
• Feels **inadequate**	• Feels **competent**
• Tries to control others and/ or becomes defiant ("You can't make me!")	• Has self-control and self- discipline
• May become dependent	• Assumes responsibility
• Seeks **power**	• Is **self-reliant**

If the child believes in his or her competence, the child behaves capably.

Children who believe they are capable can say with conviction, "I believe that I can do it."

Adolescence. Young people who develop their competence in a supportive atmosphere will develop self-control and become self-reliant. They will be able and willing to assume responsibility and enter into respectful and equal relationships. In contrast, teens who are unsure of their competence may try to prove it by taking unnecessary risks. They may resist any attempt to guide them, trying instead to show the world that they can do whatever they want and can handle whatever comes their way. Some discouraged teens take another tack and try to get others to excuse them from responsibility and give them special consideration, e.g., getting them up in the morning, picking up after them, reminding them to do their homework, repeatedly delivering forgotten lunches.

Children will *always* come up with some way to feel capable and the form it takes will be based on the choices they made earlier in life about how to connect. Sometimes people achieve only the capability of getting others to take care of them. Others may become capable by being "enablers," those who always care for others first. Becoming capable can take many forms, some clearly more satisfactory than others.

The essential need for significance; the belief that one counts

The third necessity is to feel significant, to count. All of us want to feel that we make a difference, that our existence matters. We want to believe that we will be missed if we don't show up.

Infancy. Human beings begin their lives totally self-centered. Their main occupation is to get their needs met. Developmentally, they are unable to differentiate themselves from others. Infants see others only in relation to themselves. If adults care for them and respond to their needs, they develop a feeling of security. They learn that they can count on others and that their well-being is important to their caretakers. In the early years, babies' experience of counting is pretty one-sided. They do, however, begin to make conclusions about what caring for others entails. If they are treated with consideration and respect, they will find it easier to bond with others. If they are ignored or mistreated, they may be so involved with getting their needs met that they may not be able to move beyond their own self-centered world.

Childhood. As children grow and develop their capabilities, they also try to participate in family and group life. If their attempts to take part and help out are appreciated and encouraged, they will derive their feeling of significance through membership and contribution. Their self-esteem will develop because they feel valued by others and they know that they can make a difference.

When children don't believe that they can make meaningful contributions, they may come to believe that they are insignificant. The need to feel significant is so strong that children discouraged by the belief that they can't make a difference by constructive means will find other ways to make their mark. They may give up trying to participate in helpful ways and try to prove that they count by intimidating others or by inflating their own importance by acting superior. Misbehaviors such as provoking others and seeking **revenge** are all ways of showing that they do count for something.

Adolescence. Teenagers who believe that they can make a difference in their families and in the world are eager to get involved. These young adults often become active in school and community service. They are conscious of how their behavior affects others and the world around them. They are less likely to break laws or to try to avoid responsibility because they realize that their behavior has consequences. They also see the value of voting, of developing their skills, and of participating in their community because they know that they can make a difference.

Does the child believe that he or she COUNTS in a constructive way?

The child who believes that he or she does not count in a constructive way—	The child who believes that he or she counts in a constructive way—
• Feels **insignificant** and **hurt**	• Feels **valuable**
• May try to hurt back	• Believes he or she can make a difference in a constructive way
• May seek **revenge**	• Can **contribute** constructively
• May conclude that making a negative impact is better than making no impact	

If the child believes that he or she counts in a positive way, the child behaves constructively.

Children who believe that they count in constructive ways can say with conviction, "I believe that I matter and I can make a difference."

Remember, people who don't believe that they can count through constructive means try to prove that they count through negative means. We are well aware of the dangers of that belief in adolescence. Teenage girls may become sexually active as a way of getting someone to care about them. Some have even chosen to have a baby in order to feel that someone needs them. Some teenage boys may try to get girls pregnant in order to feel that they have done something important. Vandalism and other disruptive behavior can also be ways to have an impact on those around you.

Even teens who don't actively try to prove that they count through destructive behavior are at risk. They may refuse to cooperate or to work towards any meaningful goals because they believe that nothing they do really matters. If they throw their trash out the window, who cares? It's only a little trash. Why should they care about the environment? Nobody cares anything about them. If they don't do their chores, who cares? Someone else can do them. What difference does it make if they vote? It's only one vote. Nothing ever changes anyway.

Children will always come up with some ways to feel that they count. Here again, the form it takes will be based on the choices they made earlier in life about what they must do to connect and what they are capable of. If we want our children to make constructive choices, to take their place in society, and to become good citizens, they must believe that their opinions and actions matter.

The lifelong need for courage

Human development from infancy to adulthood, and, indeed, to the end of life, is a complex and risky undertaking, a journey filled with trial and error and trial again until the person finds a way that works. It is a journey that takes a great amount of courage.

Courage, then, is the fourth of the "Crucial Cs." How important is it to leading a constructive life? It is so important that Rudolf Dreikurs often said that if we could give children only one quality to get them through life, courage would be the most necessary.

Infancy and childhood. The early signs of courage appear after every unsuccessful developmental effort the infant makes. Nothing the infant undertakes is successful on the first try except by accident, and mastery requires many, many trials.

Infants and children must possess a great amount of courage in order to keep trying to achieve what they need and want to do. This fact becomes obvious when we recall their faces and voices when they encounter major failure in their efforts (a scraped knee, a bumped head, or a buckling leg when learning to walk; the inability to make themselves understood when learning to talk; the physical and emotional hurt of falling off a bike when learning to ride).

Another way we can get some idea of the life-sustaining role courage plays in human development is to recall some of our own emotions upon confronting very difficult tasks in childhood—going to school for the first time, taking the bus or subway alone, getting lost and needing help, learning to swim. Remember the fear or perhaps terror you felt one of those times when you wanted to accomplish something very much. Did you go forward in spite of the fear? Did you give up or avoid the situation?

Hurt, anger, frustration, disappointment, and fear are all emotions human beings experience very early in life. In the course of learning, infants and children have more experiences of failure than of success. It's a wonder that they keep trying, and that wonder is called courage.

For babies and children to develop as fully as possible, they must have the courage to press on in the face of failure and fear. Courage is not the absence of fear; courage is the willingness to go forward and do what needs to be done in spite of the fear.

Children without courage focus on what they can't do. They often give up and try to **avoid** reminders of their feelings of fear and failure by getting others to give up on them, too. Infants and children with courage develop **resiliency**. They feel hopeful and are willing to take reasonable risks and try new things, and try them again after failure.

Adolescence. Adolescence is a time of great confusion and uncertainty. One foot is still in childhood, the other tentatively seeking a toehold in adulthood only to become off-balance and to land back in childhood. One step forward and two steps back, two steps forward and two steps back, then eventually two steps forward and one step back. Such is the nature of teenage progress.

The teenager probably is struggling with the time-honored problems of sexuality, the competing demands of family membership and peer-group membership, the dependence-versus-independence dilemma in its many forms, and so on. The teenager in today's society may also be struggling with the newer problems posed by the prevalence of violence, teen suicide, drugs, alcohol, dress standards, and other harsh realities.

The fear of AIDS besets some young people as they think about or engage in sexual exploration—and even worse, some don't worry about it at all. Prevalent ideas about how bodies should look may lead some to eating disorders and others to steroid usage.

The amount of courage teens need to deal with the issues that are appropriate to their age is enormous. The amount of courage required of teens who face some of the life-threatening challenges we've named here is of heroic proportions.

Does the child have COURAGE?

The child who does not have courage—	The child who has courage—
• Cannot overcome fear	• Overcomes fear
• Feels **inferior**, **defeated**, **hopeless**, and **discouraged**	• Feels **equal**, **confident**, and **hopeful**
• May give up, use **avoidance**	• Faces challenges, is **resilient**
• May be afraid to go against the crowd	• Can stand alone if necessary

If the child has courage, he or she can carry out the learning and sustain the effort that life requires.

Children with courage can say with conviction, "I believe that I can handle what comes."

Adolescents without courage don't speak in class for fear of being wrong—or, where there is a culture of disdain for school among the students, some don't speak for fear of being right. Teens who lack courage probably will not be able to resist pressure to take drugs or drink alcohol or shoplift or play with guns. Adolescents with courage have the strength they need to face life's challenges and difficulties and go against the crowd when the situation requires it. Adolescents with courage can say no to unwanted sexual advances. They can refuse to travel with the crowd when the driver has been drinking.

Essential skills and abilities

In order for the Crucial Cs to be fulfilled constructively, a person must also develop four important sets of skills.

1. **COMMUNICATION** skills. This means being able to talk, express one's self and having the willingness to listen to others. Communication is required in all of our life tasks—in making and keeping friends, on the job, and in intimate relationships. We have to be able to listen, cooperate, negotiate, share, empathize.

The number one reason people lose their jobs, other than major cutbacks, is due to poor interpersonal skills—they don't know how to get along with others. The major reason friendships break up is poor communication. When people get divorced, what do they usually give as the reason? "We couldn't communicate." What is the biggest complaint that we hear between adults and children? "You don't understand me." Without communication skills, people lose jobs and can't maintain relationships.

We need to be able to communicate effectively if we are going to CONNECT constructively.

2. **SELF-DISCIPLINE.** This means that children are able to control their emotions and behavior in order to achieve

positive goals for themselves and for the community. It means being able to work for something in the present so that they can achieve something in the future. It also means holding off getting or doing what you want right now because it might interfere with achieving your long-term goals—like not getting that expensive pair of sneakers because you're saving for college or a special trip.

Children with self-discipline are in control of themselves. They can control feelings like anger and aggression so that they don't use them self-destructively or to hurt those they care about. Children with self-discipline can put their feelings to work to motivate themselves and help change what needs to be changed. These children develop inner strength and are able to resist negative pressures and temptations. They can succeed at school and get and keep jobs. Without this characteristic people feel out of control, vulnerable, at the mercy of luck and fate.

We need self-discipline to become CAPABLE.

3. The ability and willingness to **ASSUME RESPONSIBILITY.** This means looking to see what needs to be done and doing it, setting goals, and following through. Children must learn the difference between rights and privileges, and the responsibility that goes with each.

Kids must also learn to take responsibility for their actions. They should not be able to excuse their behavior by blaming others: "It was her idea!" "He made me do it!" "They told me I should!" "I was only following orders!" or depend on others to think for them or protect them from dangers: "You should have told me before." "I thought he knew how to drive." "I thought Joanie had asked her mother to pick us up."

When children do well in school they should know it is because they did the work and when they do poorly they should be able to analyze their mistakes. They also need to look to see what can be learned from their experiences, fix what they can, and decide what they will do differently in the future. Leadership and high productivity depend on assuming responsibility. Without this ability, people tend to feel overburdened and that life is not fair.

We need to believe that we COUNT and make a difference if we are going to be willing to assume responsibility.

4. The ability to use **GOOD JUDGMENT** and **MAKE WISE DECISIONS**. This requires being open to facts and others' ideas, being able to look at options, weigh various possibilities, and make reasonable choices.

We are bombarded every day with endless choices—on grocery shelves, in shopping malls, and on television. The workplace also reflects this trend. As more and more jobs are automated, there is less need for people who are good at following orders or rote repetition. Employers want people who are able to figure things out and to think for themselves. More important, as citizens of a democracy, we are called upon to exercise judgment and make decisions about competing ideas. We must be able to decide who is trustworthy, how to vote, and what to believe. To live in today's world one must be able to make good choices. Our behavioral responses determine how we will be in relation to others—our friends, family, and the larger society—in other words, how we want and will try to live our lives.

Good judgment is essential if children are to be able to decide if something is safe or dangerous, fair or unfair, appropriate or inappropriate, moral or immoral, ethical or unethical. Children need good judgment to help decide when to go along with the group and when to stand up for what they know is right. They need to be able to decide when they should lead and when they should follow.

Today's society holds many dangers for our children. Newspapers are full of stories about kids faced with abuse, drugs, alcohol, sexual activity, and violence. We can no longer depend on adults to watch out for our children. We can't simply teach kids to always respect their elders and do what any grown-up says. We must teach them to evaluate situations, consider consequences, and decide for themselves. Without good judgment kids are more vulnerable to peer pressure, joining cults and gangs, and being taken advantage of by unscrupulous adults.

We need good judgment if we are going to use our COURAGE wisely and safely.

All of these skills are essential to academic success.

The development of these four sets of skills and qualities, which are critical to a person's life, cannot be left to chance. They *must* be cultivated and nurtured. Although nothing we can do guarantees that our children will turn out exactly the way we want them to, we *can* increase the likelihood of producing capable, well adjusted young people *if* we put thought and effort into our classroom discipline techniques.

Children may or may not arrive in the classroom having achieved a level of development appropriate to their age. Whether or not they do, there is much that teachers can do to foster this development—and the effort need not interfere with academic work, but rather can make teaching and learning more enjoyable and more effective.

Understanding Behaviors as Ways of Seeking to Fulfill Needs

All human beings strive to fulfill their needs to be connected to others, to be capable of a degree of independence, and to count as a member of the family and the community. As infants and children, we try out various behaviors to get these needs met. We learn that some behaviors get responses and some don't, and that some behaviors get better responses than others.

When constructive behaviors bring the desired results, the child incorporates those constructive behaviors into his or her fulfillment strategy. When misbehaviors bring the desired results, those misbehaviors are what gets incorporated into the child's fulfillment strategy. People may feel connected because they belong to the community or to a gang. People may feel capable of taking on responsibility or may make a career out of avoiding what is expected of them. People may feel that they count when they contribute or they may find their significance through misbehavior or self-elevation. Teen gangs and cults provide all the Crucial Cs through negative means, but for some people a gang is the only place that they feel connected and capable and that they count. (See Crucial Cs chart in the Appendix.)

Each time children succeed in getting a need met, they gain in the courage available to sustain them through the next series of trials and errors they will experience as they strive to master the next task. When children experience only failure and don't succeed in getting their needs met sufficiently, they lose some of their courage and become increasingly timid in the face of new challenges.

If we want children to get their needs met in constructive ways and to possess the courage they will need throughout their entire lives, we need to become aware of the part that we as teachers, parents, and caregivers play in the results children get from their learning efforts. Criticism and disrespect interfere with children's desire and ability to develop the courage they need to get the Crucial Cs through constructive means.

Since every behavior has a purpose, one way to understand our children is to look for the underlying purposes of their actions. We do that in terms of the Crucial Cs, looking at all behavior as a result of—

- Feeling the Crucial Cs
- Striving to feel the Crucial Cs
- Not feeling one or more of the Crucial Cs

The goals of misbehavior

We must try to determine how our children see the world and their place in it. Keep in mind that children's behavior has a purpose—is to connect, feel capable, and count in their family and later in the school and community. Problems arise because, as Dreikurs says, "Children are expert observers, but make many mistakes in interpreting what they observe. They often draw wrong conclusions and choose mistaken ways to find their place" (1964, p. 15).

Misbehavior is a symptom of these wrong conclusions.

A child who is discouraged about his or her ability to connect, feel capable, and count through constructive means develops coping strategies designed to compensate for the missing Cs. These coping strategies, which include behaviors like quitting, avoiding, cheating, clowning, bullying, controlling, forgetting, stalling, denying, rationalizing, making excuses, blaming others, and impulsivity, fall into four general categories of short-range goals that Dreikurs called the "mistaken goals of behavior." These coping strategies then are actually the misguided behaviors used to pursue mistaken goals.

Children who don't feel **connected** feel insecure and isolated and might try to prove they belong by seeking **attention**.

Children who don't feel **capable** feel inadequate. If they can't feel competent in their own right, they may choose an alternative route, mistaking power for competency. They may seek this short-range goal of **power** by trying to control others or by showing that others can't control them.

Children who don't feel as if they **count** may try to punish others for their feeling of insignificance. They may try to get **revenge** and show their pain or hurt back as they have felt hurt.

Finally, children without **courage** often feel inferior. They may use **avoidance** or assumed disability and give up in order to preserve the remnants of their damaged self-esteem.

The problem is that these goals are like candy; they provide quick satisfaction but have no long-term nourishing effect. Since they, like candy, seem to take care of the immediate discomfort, the child may not even bother to try for healthier relationships and the resultant damage may not be noticed until the damage is serious.

REMINDER: The misbehavior you see is not the problem. It's a solution to a problem the child feels he or she has. We have to help children find alternative solutions.

Instead of **connecting** by seeking undue attention, we want children to experience belonging through **cooperation**. We want children to feel **capable** and competent through **self-reliance**, not from the misuse of power. We want children to feel that they **count** and can make a difference through **contribution,** not revenge. We want children to develop **resiliency** and have the **courage** to face and overcome their difficulties, not avoid them.

To have a better picture of how these goals might manifest themselves in the classroom, imagine the following scenarios.

Mistaken goal #1: Seeking undue attention as a way to connect

Teacher: "All right, class, it's time for our math test. Clear off your desks and take out your paper and pencil."

Student fiddles in his desk for awhile, shuffles papers, drops books, then jumps up smiling and skips to the pencil sharpener.

What might the teacher say? Probably, "Please sit down!"

Student: "Oh, OK, I was just trying to get ready for the test." Knocks more stuff onto floor, giggles, adjusts clothes, smiles coyly.

How would the teacher probably feel? Irritated and annoyed.

Mistaken goal #2: Seeking power as a way to feel capable

Teacher: "All right, class, it's time for our math test. Clear off your desks and take out your paper and pencil."

Student gets up and saunters over to pencil sharpener, with smug look.

What might the teacher say? "SIT down!"

Student: "I'm just trying to get ready for the test! You do want me to take the test don't you? I can't exactly take it without a pencil, can I?"

How would the teacher probably feel? Angry or challenged.

Mistaken goal #3: Seeking revenge as a way to count
Teacher: "All right, class, it's time for our math test. Clear off your desks and take out your paper and pencil."

Student saunters over to the pencil sharpener bumping into others' desks and kicking anything on the floor on the way.

What might the teacher say? "SIT DOWN!"

Student: "Geez, I'm just getting my pencil sharpened. What do you want me to do—write with my fingers?" (Pointing to the most well behaved kid in class,) "When she got up to sharpen her pencil, you didn't yell at her. You want me to sit down? OK, I'll sit down." (Pushes another child out of a seat and sits down in it.)

How would the teacher probably feel? Attacked—tempted to punish.

Mistaken goal #4: Using avoidance to compensate for loss of courage

Teacher: "All right, class, it's time for our math test. Clear off your desks and take out your paper and pencil."

This extremely discouraged student seems to crumble and puts his head down on the desk. You wish he would sharpen a pencil.

What might the teacher say? "What's the matter? Won't you at least try?"

How would the teacher probably feel? Hopeless.

While the initial behaviors were the same in all of the preceding examples, the students' responses to correction and the teacher's feelings were different because each child's goal was different.

In order to determine a child's mistaken goal we must ask ourselves two questions:

- How do we feel when the child misbehaves?
- What is the child's response to correction?

If you feel. . .	And the student's Response is. . .	The goal is. . .
irritated, annoyed	temporarily stops	attention
angry, challenged	to escalate, to intensify	power
like punishing, or you feel hurt	to make self disliked, to hurt	revenge
despair, hopeless	to display inadequacy	avoidance

Each of the goals can be pursued through behaviors ranging from active to passive. Children can try to get your attention by actions that disrupt the group or by constantly getting you to remind them of their responsibilities. They may try to prove their power by trying to show others that, "You can't stop me!" or "You can't make me!" Children who are into revenge might show their pain by trying to hurt others or by trying to make others feel bad by showing how others have hurt them. Children may be so discouraged about their ability to measure up that their goal is to get you to give up on them. They may do this through hyperactive behavior or by overemphasizing their learning disabilities. Although these children may or may not be correctly labeled or diagnosed, not all children with these diagnoses display their inadequacies and give up. We all know people who have developed strategies to compensate for these problems and have gone on to achieve great things. For example, Einstein was dyslexic and we can only imagine what it would have been like to have had the exuberant antics of the comedian, Robin Williams, in your class.

Confirming the student's goal

Although children are not consciously aware of the purpose of their behavior, they can recognize their goals when they are pointed out in a friendly and helpful manner. To check out your hypothesis about the purpose of the student's behavior and to help the child understand why he or she is behaving in a self-defeating way, the teacher can use the following format for goal disclosure.

Warning: Goal disclosure is only to confirm your thoughts and to help the student feel understood. Be sure your goal is to help the child understand, not to punish or accuse. If you can not be sure that you are feeling empathy for this child, do not attempt the conversation.

At a time other than when the student is misbehaving, ask in a friendly tone:

1. Do you know why you daydream and look out the window during class discussions? (Be specific when you describe the misbehavior. Don't just say, "Why do you misbehave in class?") The child will probably say "No," or come up with some excuse. (If the student does try to give a reason, you can say, "That may be so but I have another idea.")

2. "May I tell you what I think?" It is important to ask for permission so that the student doesn't feel accused. When the atmosphere is friendly and children are not concerned with defending themselves, they will usually be curious to hear what you think.

3. At this time we go through the following sequence of questions in order to confirm our hypothesis about the child's mistaken goal and to help the child recognize the purpose of the misbehavior. Children will respond with what Rudolf Dreikurs called a "recognition reflex" when we have correctly identified the goal. A recognition reflex can take many forms. One child might simply say, "Yes." Another child might say, "No," but show by a smile or some other body language that this explanation is correct. Sometimes you will get a weak recognition with one question and a much stronger response to the next, but if the suggested purpose is not correct for this child, there will be no recognition reflex at all.

The first question we ask should always be related to Goal 1, Attention Getting behavior. "Could it be that you would like people to notice you?" or "Could it be that you would like more of my time?"

Goal 2, Power, is identified by asking, "Could it be that you want to show people that you can do what you want?" (active) or "Could it be that you want to show people that they can't make you do what they want? (passive)

The next question pertains to Goal 3, Revenge, and is uncovered by asking, "Could it be that you sometimes feel that others are hurting you and you want to show them how it feels by hurting them back?" or "Could it be that you feel others treat you unfairly and you want to get even?"

The final question is directed at Goal 4, Avoidance. This highly discouraged child can be asked, "Could it be that you're convinced that you will never measure up and you would rather not try at all and perhaps you wish people would just leave you alone?"

Why is the goal important?

If you went to a doctor complaining of a pain in your chest, you would expect her to do an examination, determine the problem, and come up with a treatment plan that was appropriate to you. We all know that the same symptom can be present in different illnesses. A pain in the chest can be a sign of indigestion, pneumonia, a heart problem, or anxiety. If we try to treat the symptom without determining the underlying problem, we would be ineffective, at best; at worst we might cause even more damage.

Just like the doctor, if we want to effectively respond to a child's misbehavior we must first determine the underlying problem not just react to the symptom. We can see this from the examples of the students sharpening the pencil, one child might disturb the class because he wants to be the center of attention. Another child may try to disrupt the class because she wants to show you that she can do what she wants or that you can't make her do what you want. She wants to show her power. Another student may become disruptive because he feels he doesn't count except when he is causing trouble. This child feels hurt and wants to get even by getting revenge. And finally, a child may not feel capable of meeting any challenges and he wants you to give up and stop asking. This child is trying to protect his self-esteem by avoidance or display of inadequacy.

As you can see, the same behavior can have very different goals, and different goals require different methods for correction. This explains why some techniques work for awhile and then stop being effective, or work with some children or some classes but not others. In order to know what to do, we must have some idea of what the underlying problem is, not just the symptom.

How does the child develop mistaken goals?

The four goals of misbehavior are mistaken approaches to trying to achieve the Crucial Cs. Children using a process of trial and error try to figure out ways to connect, feel capable, and count. They try different behaviors, keeping the ones that seem to work and discarding the others.

Mistaken goal #1:
Demanding attention instead of seeking constructive connection

The most common error occurs when a child discovers that it feels good to get attention. The child may reason that getting attention is a good way to be sure of belonging, of being connected. At this critical point, children may get the mistaken idea that the only way to be sure of belonging is to keep others busy meeting their needs or at least not let others be busy with something or someone else. Such reasoning results in a demand for too much attention. Of course, we all need attention, but a demand for exclusive or full-time attention, though reasonable by the child's standards, is not realistic, appropriate, or acceptable.

In an attempt to appease children who seek attention instead of constructive connection, adults often act as if attention were a cup that can be filled and that when it is full, the child will say, "Thanks, I've had enough. Why don't you go do your work now?" But this cup has a hole in the bottom. We can keep adding more, but we can't ever fill the cup. Children with the mistaken goal of getting attention never get "enough." They soon forget the attention they have already gotten because it's the attention they *don't* get that is important to them. When the demand is total, nothing less will do.

Dealing with a student who is constantly seeking attention is like trying to have a serious conversation with someone who is wearing a funny hat and hopping around: it simply can't be done. Although the child's distracting behavior may not be as troublesome as some other student's misbehavior, the constant disruptions quickly become annoying and irritating.

When these children disturb the class, forget things, interrupt, etc., we usually do the wrong thing in response. We notice the misbehavior and give them the attention they demand. "I've told you sixteen times you may not interrupt." What has the child just done sixteen times? Interrupted us. And what have we done sixteen times? Given them undue attention.

What we want is for the child to learn that she is important even when we are busy doing something else. If she feels secure in her connection she can find her place through cooperation. The way to guide her in that direction is to ignore the attention-demanding misbehavior and give attention for appropriate behavior.

As with all mistaken goals, the student's attention seeking usually provokes negative feelings in the teacher. We often are tempted to try to change children and convince them that they are wrong. This only creates defensiveness and may make matters worse. Instead, we need to change *our response* to the misbehavior. Children remember and retain the behaviors that adults react to; children abandon those behaviors to which adults don't respond. To deal with the frustration and annoyance associated with attention-seeking behavior, it is helpful to imagine the child wearing a sign that says, "I WANT TO CONNECT. CATCH ME BEING GOOD."

Once we begin to understand the student's behavior in a different way, we can change our responses. We can stop reinforcing mistaken goals and begin to guide the child to more constructive approaches for connecting to others. The basic principle is to modify our response to the student's behavior based on an understanding of the child's goal. Here are some effective strategies for redirecting the student's behaviors—

1. **Minimize the attention given to misbehavior**. We don't have to notice every slight transgression. Remember that children repeat behaviors that get the desired response. Children who are driven by the desire for attention would rather be reprimanded than ignored.

2. **Notice the behaviors you want to encourage.** Focus on contributions, working well with others, cooperation, and other constructive behaviors.
3. **Act *before* there is a problem.** We are often tempted to leave children alone when they are behaving appropriately and only step in when there is a problem. However logical that approach may seem, it doesn't work; that approach misses the opportunities to notice constructive behavior and reinforces the idea that misbehavior gets attention. Instead, we should give children attention when they are not demanding it.
4. **Act, don't talk!** If you see a child beginning to disrupt the class, instead of reprimanding and drawing more attention to her, you can move to her vicinity, perhaps put your hand on her shoulder and use your presence to connect.
5. **Give jobs that get positive attention by being helpful to others**—like collecting papers, handing out crayons, doing a math problem at the board. In this way the students learn that they don't have to misbehave in order to get attention and we can redirect them towards cooperative behavior.

In the case of the pencil sharpener, the teacher might address the group. "Class, we have ten minutes to finish the work." In this way you can address the situation, not the individual.

Mistaken goal #2: Seeking power instead of capability

Children have many years to try out ways to become capable of caring for themselves, but self-reliance is not always the result of their efforts. When children compare themselves to parents or older siblings, for example, they may not realize that they will grow and develop their own competencies. They may decide that they don't measure up and are in an inferior position. The child may try to compensate for the feeling of powerlessness by trying to be "more powerful" than others.

The first signs of the power goal may show up as the "terrible two's." When the child first begins to experience the power of language and the word "no," the child practices it at every opportunity. If parents respond to these first signs of autonomy by trying to make the child cooperate, he may become convinced that important people in this world are able to make others do as they say. If the child doesn't feel successful at bossing others, he can at least show them that they can't boss him. What's more powerful than defeating the most powerful people in your life?

Since everyone wants to feel "empowered" in some way, when we don't provide children with the opportunity to develop their competencies and become self-reliant, they may get the wrong idea about being "powerful." We all want our students to become responsible and to feel capable, but in our haste to get through the curriculum and fit in all the other things we must do each day we may not take the time to teach our students to be responsible for themselves. It may be tempting to remind students of their obligations and tell them what to do and how to do it, but it doesn't encourage self-reliance.

Teaching a student who is seeking power is like trying to have a relationship with someone who only wants to fight with you or defeat you. We are usually tempted to do the wrong thing in response to the challenging display of power. We get so angry at this child that we want to "show him that he can't get away with this!" Of course, what we are actually doing is impressing the child with *our* power and showing him that he may need to work even harder to defeat us. He may decide to go undercover and resist passively, by forgetting, not listening, or failing at school; or he may decide to pick on those who are smaller or weaker.

What we should do in this situation is what Rudolf Dreikurs suggested, instead of trying to take the wind out of his sail, we should take our sail out of his wind (1964, p. 155). He can keep on blowing, but we will not be pushed around. In this way we show the child that we *refuse to fight* with him, and we *refuse to give in* to his unreasonable demands.

Once we begin to understand the student's display of power in a different way, our anger begins to dissipate and we are able to change our responses. We can stop reinforcing this mistaken goal and begin to guide the child to more constructive approaches for feeling capable. Here are some effective strategies for redirecting students' behaviors towards seeking to develop their competence:

1. **Think about what *you* can do rather then what *they* should do.**
2. **When correcting a misbehaving student, focus on the behavior, not the child.** While a child's actions may be unacceptable, the child never is.
3. **Don't escalate.** Refuse to be drawn into a struggle for power. If you fight with the child, he or she may decide to resist in order to save face.
4. **Give this student real responsibilities to let him or her know that you think the child is capable.** In this way the child becomes empowered through constructive means. (Remember to give choices and involve the child in decision making.)
5. **Whenever possible decide on rules and consequences as a class.** In this way you can avoid

being set up as the authority to be defeated. If a student breaks an agreed-upon rule, it is the class the child is challenging and not a teacher.

In the case of the pencil sharpener the teacher might ask, "While you're over there, would you please sharpen these pencils for me?" In this way the teacher turns the invitation to a fight into an opportunity for the student to make a contribution. If the student is really angry, he will probably say, "Do it yourself!" The teacher doesn't need to respond.

Mistaken goal #3: Seeking revenge in order to count

In our society there is little chance for a child to make a useful contribution. In earlier times, it was important that each person do his part. Everyone's survival depended on it; if you didn't bring in the wood there was no heat; if you forgot to gather the eggs there was no breakfast. Today, we give children jobs with little status, like taking out the garbage, and when they forget we nag and remind them and often do the job ourselves. Even such personal responsibilities as doing homework and remembering lunch money and boots often become the adult's job. It is little wonder that kids don't see their contributions as important, and often believe that adults' requests for cooperation are simply arbitrary means for controlling them.

If a child becomes so discouraged that she feels that she is not needed, cannot be liked, or cannot get her way, she may move to the goal of revenge. This child believes that her only chance to prove that she counts is by seeking revenge and hurting others as she has felt hurt.

This behavior can be expected from children who have been neglected, abused, or overpowered. However, revenge is often a response of a pampered child as well. This child has been raised to believe that she has a right to special attention and when she doesn't get it, she has the right to punish those who deprived her of her "birthright."

A child who resorts to revenge is one of the most difficult to work with. She will often push you until you get mad or upset and then she says, "See, I knew you didn't like me." Teachers and parents may think that a little more attention will turn this child around, but the more the adult gives, the more the child escalates until the adult gives up in frustrated anger and hurt. Trying to teach this child is like interacting with someone who is covered with mouse traps which are always baited, ready to catch you before you can hurt her.

Before you can figure out what to do you must realize that the child's goal is to prove that the world is unfair and she wants to punish others for the injustice that she suffers. The first step in dealing with revenge is to try to rebuild the relationship. However, adults must act swiftly to maintain their self-respect and protect their own rights while not humiliating the child or infringing on the child's rights.

Adults who are confronted with a child who is trying to hurt them are tempted to hurt back and punish. One way to keep from getting caught up in the cycle of revenge is to remind yourself of the child's great pain and discouragement. It is sometimes helpful to imagine the student wearing a sign that says: I WANT TO COUNT. FIND SOMETHING TO LIKE ABOUT ME. I'M HURTING.

To help fight your own discouragement it is important to remember that this goal of relationship building underlies all of the suggested strategies. This will not be easy, as the child's goal is to prove that you do not care. Although you may be tempted to show the child how bad she is, this is not necessary. She's already convinced that others feel this way. Your job is to convince her otherwise and to get her to believe in herself. One way to do this is to enlist the aid of other staff members (teachers, secretaries, and janitors). Explain that this child is at risk and you would like their help in encouraging her. Ask them to go out of their way to make some positive comment or connection with her. Warn them that she may sabotage their efforts. You may have to brainstorm together to find the hidden good beneath the obvious misbehavior.

You may want to enlist the aid of the school counselor or psychologist, who might decide that a referral to an outside professional is warranted.

Our own hurt feelings become more bearable once we are able to see the child's deep discouragement. If we can put her hurtful behavior into context, then we can stop reinforcing her mistaken perceptions. Only then can we begin to guide the child to more constructive approaches for feeling that she counts. Here are some effective strategies:

1. **Make a list of positives about this child** and refer to it often, especially when you're feeling defeated. Share the list with your colleagues and ask them to contribute to it.
2. **Refuse to retaliate, escalate, or humiliate**. Maintain a respectful relationship. Act before you get angry. Avoid focusing on every small transgression. Choose your conflicts carefully.
3. **Before trying to resolve conflicts, allow for a cooling off period** to remind yourself that this child who is hurting you is actually feeling hurt herself.

4. **Offer lots of chances to help others,** and let the child know that his or her contributions are necessary. This child knows about injustice and will often be willing to help those less fortunate.
5. **Share responsibility for solving problems.** Ask the child, "What do you think we should do about this situation?"

In the case of the pencil sharpener, the teacher might say, "I'm glad to see that you are getting ready for the test."

Mistaken goal #4: Using avoidance due to diminished courage.

This last goal has been called avoidance of failure and displayed or assumed inadequacy. It describes the child who is convinced that he cannot succeed and cannot have power. He decides that his best chance to preserve his self-esteem is to get others to give up on him; at least this way he avoids situations where he might be humiliated. This child's goal is to be left alone to suffer in private, and to daydream about what might have been. He may think, "I'd prefer you think I am lazy rather than give you proof I am stupid." or "If I don't try, I'm not really a failure."

This child may slip into the background and may be overlooked. He may even be labeled hyperactive or learning disabled. Whether or not the diagnosis is correct is less important than the feelings of hopelessness that are elicited in the people who interact with him. Teachers and parents, discouraged about any possibility of improvement, often give up trying to get him involved. Professional help may be necessary to help counteract the despair of both the child and the people he interacts with. It is essential that this child have someone in his life who refuses to give up hope.

With this child we must really focus on encouragement. He must be convinced that the real world is better than the world of daydreams. It's awfully lonely in that world. We must try to give him a sense of belonging, show him that he is liked and that he has something to offer which is valued. By experiencing success this child begins to get the courage to try again. (Failure to accomplish usually comes from fear of failure, not laziness.)

When you find yourself feeling hopeless and discouraged, try to imagine this child wearing a sign that says:
DEVELOP MY COURAGE. BELIEVE IN ME. DON'T GIVE UP.

Discouraged children are usually surrounded by discouraged adults. Developing a manageable plan will be encouraging to both. Here are some strategies for building courage:

1. **Make mistakes a learning experience.** Point out that one must risk failure in order to develop new skills. Ask, "What will you do differently next time?" Be sure to accept your own mistakes. In order to demonstrate the importance of perseverance and learning from experience, share stories about people the child knows who have recovered from mistakes. For example, Edison had 9000 failed attempts at finding the right filament before he found one that worked, and Disney went bankrupt four times before Disneyland was a success.
2. **Create situations where success is probable.** Divide larger tasks into many more manageable steps with benchmarks to reflect progress. Provide an encouraging tutor if necessary.

3. **Recognize any effort or small improvement.** Make sure this applies to everyone in the family and not just this child. We sometimes only acknowledge perfection. This is only encouraging to those who consistently do superior work. Those who don't feel they will be successful may give up altogether. By focusing on improvement for everyone in the class we make it clear that what is important is that people work to their potential.
4. **Teach positive self-talk**. Listen to these children and what they are saying about themselves. Don't allow them to discourage themselves further with negative statements. If you hear them say, "I can't," encourage them to change it to, "I haven't learned how to do this yet." If they say, "I'm stupid," separate the person from what he or she does. Respond with, "Making mistakes doesn't mean you're stupid—making mistakes means you're learning."
5. **Don't give up.**

In the case of the pencil sharpener, the teacher might suggest, "I want you to pick one problem that you can work on. We'll talk about the rest of them later."

Changing our perceptions

While these suggestions certainly make sense, they are not easy to implement. When we are confronted with a student's misbehavior throughout the day it's difficult to avoid responding with annoyance, anger, hurt, and despair. In our concern with stopping misbehavior we often overuse consequences and lose sight of the long-range goals of developing courage, building relationships, and inviting cooperation.

Remember: Our object should not be to take the goal away since the child believes that his security is dependent upon it. Instead, we should try to redirect the child in more useful and constructive directions.

Attention:	We want the child's desire for **attention** to become an appropriate bid for acknowledgment, contact, or recognition.
Power:	We want the use of **power** to be channeled into leadership. We want this child to develop a sense of being capable through independence and self-control, not through rebellion and resistance.
Revenge:	Instead of **revenge** we want this child to focus on justice and fairness for everyone.
Avoidance:	We want this child to safeguard his self-esteem, but through the development of self-respect and courage, not through **avoidance** of daily tasks.

(See mistaken goals chart in Appendix.)

Developing Self-Esteem through Encouragement

Self-esteem is based on the feelings and thoughts that individuals possess about their sense of competence and worth, about their abilities to make a difference, to meet and overcome challenges, to learn from both success and failure, and to view themselves and others with dignity and respect.

In order to increase the likelihood that we can positively influence a child's self-esteem, motivation, and courage, we must develop the art of encouragement.

Encouragement versus evaluative praise

Encouragement means instilling courage by helping people see their strengths and develop belief in themselves. High self-esteem is related to the belief that if we work hard and keep trying we will develop the skills we need to feel successful. While experts in the past extolled the value of using praise to raise children's self-esteem, current research shows that praise frequently has the opposite effect fostering a "fixed mindset" (Dweck, 2006) based on the belief that you are either born smart or talented or not and there is little that you can do to change it. True self-esteem requires a "growth mindset" which is based on the belief that effort and motivation leads to developing the skills one needs to succeed. Commenting on improvement and effort is more encouraging than only noticing when a job is successfully completed. When we praise we are usually pointing out what we think someone already does well. There are several problems with this approach:

- By our focusing primarily on what children already do well, they may get the erroneous idea that success is the most important value. They may decide to avoid working in any area where success is not already guaranteed. Any chance of failure must be avoided because it would mean that you are not "good enough." True success, however, is usually dependent upon the willingness to put forth the effort needed to improve.
- When we focus on what the adults think rather than encouraging self-evaluation, we may actually be teaching children to become dependent on others' opinions. While we may like it when children try to please us, we worry about peer pressure when they are more concerned with gaining their friends' approval.
- The absence of consistent praise may be considered failure or proof that one is not good enough.

Encouragement	**Evaluative Praise**
an attitude	a verbal reward
task - or situation-centered	person-centered
emphasizes effort and improvement	earned by being superior
may be given during task	job must be well done/completed
shows acceptance	is judgmental
fosters independence	fosters dependence
emphasizes self-evaluation	emphasizes others' opinions
develops self-esteem	develops self-consciousness

Helping Children to Feel the Crucial Cs

The best way to encourage students and help them to develop their self-esteem is by helping them to feel the Crucial Cs through constructive means. Following are some useful tips.

Helping the student feel connected

1. Provide many opportunities for cooperative interaction.
   A. Develop class rules and problem solve at classroom meetings.
   B. Use cooperative games, plays, songs, creative dramatics. (Helping should not be seen as cheating.)
   C. Use group projects; let different groups plan a meeting or surprise for the class.
   D. Develop a group identity (create banners, songs, celebrations, class diary).
   E. Use cooperative learning activities.

2. Show an interest in each student.
   A. Be sure to greet each one by name.
   B. Acknowledge their moods—"Looks like you're having a hard day. Want to talk about it?" "You look awfully pleased today. What's up?"
   C. Chat with them in the halls, join them for lunch occasionally.
   D. Find out about hobbies, families, trips, things of interest.
   E. Ask each child to share at class meeting or teach a skill to others.

3. Give positive attention.
   A. Have a few times available each week for kids to sign up for special time.
   B. If a child wants your attention and you are busy, arrange a time to talk.
   C. Display a variety of students' work, not just perfect papers.

4. Find and recognize strengths and talents.
   A. Look for strengths—not just academic, but mechanical, artistic, athletic, creative, social.
   B. Be a talent scout—Find something the child is good at and uncover the skills used in that activity. Then show how these qualities are used in other areas. For example, What does it take to be good in math? Logic, some memorization, concentration, practice, stick-to-itiveness, being a good detective. These same skills are evident in games like dungeons and dragons, athletics, and other hobbies.
   C. As the old song suggests, "Accentuate the positive, Eliminate the negative."

5. Show acceptance—separate the deed from the doer.
   A. With both positive and negative behaviors
   B. **Be specific**—I liked the way you handled ______. I liked it when you___ because ______. When you ________, I felt _______ because __________.

6. Send cards, messages, homework to absent students.

7. Conduct classroom meetings and the Open Circle.

Helping the student feel capable

1. Make mistakes a learning experience.
   A. Set the tone on the first day of school: Ask, "How many people think they might make a mistake this year? If someone makes a mistake what do you think we should do? Who worries that you'll be asked a question and won't know the answer? If someone makes a mistake, how many think we should make fun of him or her?"
   B. Demonstrate learning from mistakes. Ask, "What did you learn from it? What will you do differently next time?"
   C. Follow Piaget's advice—look for logic behind an answer. Find out why a child answers the way she or he does (the answer may be incorrect but it is rarely illogical.) "How did you come up with this? What did you think that I meant? What would you have said if you thought I meant_____? When you did that, what did you think would happen? Did you learn anything new or surprising? What will you do next time?"
   D. Note the way you respond to errors. Allowing children time to try again, offering clues, and suggesting alternatives conveys that errors are a part of the learning process. Calling on another student

immediately conveys the message that errors are failures and we are interested in performance, not process.

E. Look for analytical ability, critical thinking, good judgment, effort, improvement, how far the person has come, not how far they have to go.

F. Concentrate on the effort, not the errors. We need to be willing to accept mistakes if we want children to risk trying new things. Creative ideas are often built on a so-called mistake.

G. Point out what is done well when grading papers. Mark tests by writing the score of the correct answers at the top of the paper. (for example, +70 instead of -30).

2. Build confidence.
   A. Focus on improvement not perfection.
   B. Notice contributions.
   C. Build on strengths.
   D. Believe in the students.
      (1) Have realistic expectations
      (2) Allow them to struggle and succeed if the job is within their capabilities. Don't feel sorry for or save; both are disrespectful and discouraging.
      (3) Acknowledge the difficulty of the situation.
      (4) Focus on the present, not the past (expecting repeat of old behaviors), or the future (kids worry about their ability to keep it up).
   E. Analyze successes to see what they did right. Why was an approach successful? Would they be willing to teach others?
   F. Insure successes--divide up large tasks into smaller more manageable ones. Give opportunities to repeat successful experiences.

3. Conduct classroom meetings and the Open Circle.

Helping the student feel he or she counts

1. Through contribution
   A. Provide opportunities for students to be helpful to the group in class.
      (1) Offer jobs that are meaningful. Give positions of responsibility.
      (2) Provide choices of projects—brainstorm:
         (a.) What could we do?
         (b.) What do we need to do it?
         (c.) How can we get what we need? ?
         (d.) Who can do what part?
      (3) Invite input into scheduling (when to hand in a paper or take a test—Friday or Monday, etc.).
      (4) Make rules together.
         (a) HELPS—Behaviors that make being here easy and fun.
         (b) HURTS—Behaviors that sabotage or interfere with others rights to play, participate, learn, or feel safe (Albert, 1989).
   B. By helping each other. Use peer tutoring.
      (1) Make a list of "Skills I am willing to teach" and "Things I would like to learn."
      (2) Brainstorm what kids would like to learn: knitting, clay, jump rope, basketball, etc.
      (3) Ask or identify who is good at specific skills (Teacher can encourage a discouraged child by identifying a valuable talent).
   C. By helping in the community.
      (1) Charity drives, community cleanup projects, etc.
      (2) Regular visitation of nursing homes, volunteering at shelters.
      (3) Tutoring younger children.

(4) Participating in schoolwide decision-making and problem-solving.

2. Through recognition.
   A. Recognition Box—Have kids fill out cards (signed or anonymous) on something they did that they're proud of or something positive they noticed about someone else.
   B. Ask students to periodically evaluate themselves, develop goals, and assess improvement.
   C. Give appreciations and compliments at Classroom Meetings.
   D. Send notes of encouragement to parents telling them about their child's improvements or continued effort.

3. Conduct classroom meetings and the Open Circle.

Helping the student develop courage

1. Have the courage to be imperfect: don't expect perfection of self or others.

2. Point to strengths, not weaknesses.

3. Don't make comparisons with others.

4. Ask questions (Do you understand? Do you need help? Is this what you meant?) in order to
   A. Encourage active participation.
   B. See if the child's understanding is the same as yours.
   C. Learn where help and/or correction are necessary.

5. Ask yourself these questions:
   A. Am I inspiring self-evaluation or dependence on other's evaluation?
   B. Am I respectful or am I patronizing?

C. Am I seeing the child's point of view or only my own?
D. Would I say this to a friend?

6. Avoid debilitating help, such as
   A. Overlooking misbehavior without taking appropriate action.
   B. Regularly doing for children what the children can do for themselves.
   C. Rescuing kids from uncomfortable consequences of their actions. (We have to intervene whenever a situation is dangerous or if the outcome would be extreme discouragement, but discomfort isn't dangerous!)

7. Avoid criticism.
   A. You must have a relationship with people if you want them to hear what you say without defensiveness (even then, it's tough).
   B. Check out what they are asking for. Is it encouragement or correction? Do they want you to give feedback on ideas or presentation? Are they asking if there are holes in the back of their shirt, or are they asking if you like the outfit?

8. Conduct classroom meetings and the Open Circle.

Logical Classroom Discipline

Schools, as well as families, have an obligation to educate children to become responsible citizens. Children need to learn that true freedom can only exist within a social order. Rudolf Dreikurs said, "Freedom is part of democracy; but the subtle point that we cannot have freedom unless we respect the freedom of others is seldom recognized. In order for everyone to have freedom, we must have order and order bears with it certain restrictions and obligations. Freedom also implies responsibility" (1964, p. 9). Without certain limits no one can feel secure and without the opportunity for choice no one can be free. Imagine how frightening it would be to cross the Golden Gate Bridge if it had no guard rails. Although we try not to bump into the railing, we feel secure knowing that it's there.

We must give students the opportunity to experience the consequences of their actions and to learn from their mistakes. Lecturing, warnings and punishment can backfire and interfere with the learning process. Students may be so angered, hurt, or distracted by our reactions to their misbehavior that they miss the real lesson—that their behavior is inappropriate, dangerous, or ineffective. Students might also decide that the only reason they shouldn't misbehave is because it gets us mad or that misbehavior is okay as long as you don't get caught.

The lesson children learn should always underscore the connection between their behavior and its results. It is helpful, therefore, to make a distinction between punishment and logical consequences. Punishment is an arbitrary consequence, designed to teach through discomfort or pain, either physical or psychological. It seems to be based on the assumption that students learn best by *suffering* the consequences of their behavior. Logical consequences, on the other hand, are based on the assumption that students learn best by experiencing the results of their behavior.

The object of discipline is to guide the child towards self-discipline, self-control; to help the child to see what should be done and what should not be done; and to take responsibility for whatever choice he or she makes.

The major differences between consequences and punishment are

	Punishment	Logical Consequences
Teaches:	Arbitrary power External control	Cooperation Self-discipline
Adult's emotion:	Anger	Friendly, concerned
Adult's action is:	Hurting Arbitrary Often impulsive	Seeking agreement Related to behavior Thoughtful, deliberate
Adult's focus:	On the past (what happened) On what CAN'T be done	On the future (what needs to be done) On what CAN be done
Child feels:	Belittled, inferior	Capable, respected
Child remembers:	Injustice, humiliation	Personal contribution Connection between behavior and results
Purpose:	Control over others	Self-control

A logical consequence must pass the test of the "3 Rs." It should be

1. **Related** logically to the misbehavior;
2. **Respectful** in order to avoid any humiliation, and be both firm (to show respect for self) and kind (to show respect for the child);
3. **Reasonable** so that it is as logically understandable to the child as to the adult. A harsh or angry consequence is always perceived as a punishment.

Classroom Meetings: An Essential Tool for Preparing Students to Thrive In a Dangerous World

It has become disturbingly clear that we can no longer act as if school is a safe sanctuary, where teachers can expect automatic respect and focus only on academics. The recent examples of deadly shootings in schools, at all levels, have brought to the forefront the need to deal with the underlying problems of alienation, bullying, feelings of inadequacy and poor social skills. These distressing concerns have a grave impact on students' ability to learn and teachers' ability to teach.

The good news is that classroom meetings, held on a regular basis, not only help teachers learn what is going on in the minds of their students but can provide an opportunity for counteracting these feelings while fostering the perceptions and skills students will need to thrive in an ever more dangerous world. Furthermore, children who internalize the Crucial Cs, and develop the essential skills of communication, assuming responsibility and exercising self-discipline and good judgment are more successful in school and have what it takes to become responsible, contributing citizens in society.

Group discussions and classroom meetings are the best vehicles to teach social logic and democratic principles. Since these skills are also necessary for academic success, time spent in their development will be time well spent.

Classroom Meetings

The format of the Classroom Meeting can be adapted for many purposes. It can be used to:

1. **Give compliments and appreciations.** This item comes at the beginning of the meeting to set the tone for pleasant communication. Criticism and complaints are commonplace in most schools. If we want to change the atmosphere in the classroom we can begin by teaching students how to lift each other up rather than put each other down.

   Pointing to a person's strengths is an important part of building self-confidence and courage. We often find ourselves complimenting only those who are already successful. Children who consistently misbehave rarely hear people speak about what they do right. They may become so discouraged that they decide that the only way others will notice them is if they cause trouble.

2. **Develop classroom rules together**. Teachers can lead students in a discussion about the importance of rules. (What would happen if we had no rules? When do rules help? When do they interfere? What can you do if you think a rule is unfair?). This discussion could be related to social studies topics such as the differences between anarchy, monarchy, dictatorship and democracy and how it would feel to live in each.

   No matter what additional rules your class may suggest, we recommend at least two that underscore the logic of social living:
   A. Respect self and others.
   B. Help each other.

3. **Address problems**. The classroom meeting should be a place where each student can receive help and can be of help to others. Concerns and conflicts may be placed on an agenda (see below). Rudolf Dreikurs said, "The crucial factor is the shared responsibility, a process of thinking

through the problems which come up for discussion, and an exploration about alternatives. Shared responsibility is best accomplished with the question, 'What can we do about it?" (1957, p. 185)

4. **Encourage reflection.** Teachers can use this time to pose questions about larger issues and provide a safe space for children to think about behavior and hear others' opinions. Questions can cover things like, Why do people bully other people? What would you do if all your friends were encouraging you to do something that you didn't think was right? What is peer pressure? Why does it work? What can you do if you don't want to go along? What would you do if you saw someone picking on someone else? This also gives teachers an invaluable insight into what their students think.

5. **Share information.** Time should be set aside to discuss upcoming events, class trips, birthdays, etc. In order to increase students' sense of responsibility they should be included in the decision-making process. One way to do this is to allow them input into scheduling of assignments, exams, or projects. Although students may not decide whether or not they have exams or projects, it is often beneficial to include them in the decision about when they will occur (e.g., before or after weekends or holidays).

6. **Decide on contributions to the classroom and school community**. The meeting could be a time when class jobs are chosen and rotated. Students might also discuss ways they could serve the school community (tutoring, clean-up and planting flowers, community service projects, etc.).

At regularly scheduled Classroom Meetings students get a chance to learn first hand, through experience and observation, all of the perceptions, skills, and abilities that they need to develop the Crucial Cs through useful means:

Connect. Each person is given the opportunity to identify with and take responsibility for the group process. Each student is guaranteed acceptance, a chance to be heard and taken seriously.
Capable. Compliments, appreciations, problem-solving, and decision-making components of the meeting point out strengths and help all students see that they are competent.
Count. Students can see that what they do makes a difference and that they are capable of making necessary contributions.
Courage. Through problem solving and evaluating outcomes students learn they can discuss their problems openly, learn from their mistakes, and try again.
Communication. Everyone is given a chance to speak and to be heard. Students are taught how to listen and learn to respect others by not interrupting. Everyone hears how others share ideas and feelings. Cooperation, empathy, respect, and negotiation are modeled and practiced so that children learn how to communicate in ways that invite others to listen.
Good judgment. The group discusses the significance of their experiences. Problems are identified and analyzed. Various solutions are tried and examined to see how they will affect each member and to determine if they are respectful to self and others. Choices are given and consequences are experienced.
Responsibility. Everyone is given a chance to contribute to the class. All students are asked to take a turn leading meetings, taking notes of the proceedings, and participating in non-leadership roles. Choices,

consequences, freedom, and limits are given to all. Solutions are solicited from everyone.
Self-discipline. Rules and consequences are decided upon by all. All members get to experience the consequences of their actions. Everyone gives and receives feedback.

The Meder-Platt model for Classroom Meetings

Frank Meder, a former elementary school teacher and intern trainer, and John Platt, a counselor, in Sacramento, California, developed an effective system for Classroom Meetings.

Students are taught to list any problem or issue they have in an agenda book that is available for students to use. Twice a week, at a scheduled time, the students quickly form a circle with their chairs and address problems together.

This model uses the following steps:

1. Compliments, statements of appreciation, thank yous
   Students are taught how to encourage others by giving compliments or expressing appreciation. The teacher goes around the circle calling on anyone who has a hand raised and wants to compliment or show appreciation for another student or group of students. Students who receive compliments or appreciations respond by saying, "Thank you" or "You're welcome."

2. Problems
   a. Using the agenda book the teacher calls on the first person whose name appears in the book and reads the problem listed, followed by the question: "Jim, is this still important?" If Jim says, "No," the teacher goes to the next item listed on the agenda.

b. If Jim says, "Yes," the teacher continues by stating the problem and asking the class, "How many people like it when this happens to them?" and "How many people don't like it when this happens to them?"

This quick tabulation is an instantaneous and powerful way to poll the group for opinions on socially acceptable or unacceptable behaviors. Instead of feeling criticized by the teacher, a student is able to see how a behavior impacts on others.

c. If the complaint has been lodged against another student, that child is asked, "Susie, what do you think should be done about this? Do you have any ideas?"

This question shows respect for the person who will be affected by the decision. No one is excluded from taking responsibility and this student is invited to share expertise and judgment about appropriate consequences.

d. If Susie makes a suggestion, the class is asked, "How many think this is a helpful suggestion?" If the majority of the class thinks the suggestion is acceptable, that suggestion is used. If not, the class is asked, "How many think this is not a helpful suggestion?"

e. If Susie's suggestion is unacceptable, Jim is asked if he has an idea to recommend that would be helpful to Susie. Then other possibilities are solicited from class members. (In order for a solution to be considered, the class is trained to make suggestions that are *related* to the incident, *reasonable*, and *respectful*. All suggestions should help students assume *responsibility* for their actions.) To keep things manageable, usually no more than five suggestions are accepted for consideration.

f. The suggestions are read and the class is asked to vote for the one they think would be most helpful to Susie. The idea that gets the most votes is the one selected.

g. Susie is given a choice about when the solution will be applied. For instance, if the solution is to have Susie skip a recess due to inappropriate playground behavior, the teacher will ask Susie if she wants to skip the next recess or the following recess. This is one way of ensuring that the child will not be discounted, ignored, or left out of any of the steps that will affect her.

h. The class is then asked if anyone has any tips for Susie so that she doesn't run into this problem again.

A video and training guide describing the Meder/ Platt model for conducting classroom meetings may be purchased through Dynamic Training & Seminars, 8902 Quartzite Circle, Granite Bay, California 94746, telephone 800-262-4387.

The Reach Out to Schools—Social Competency Program: The Open Circle

The Reach Out to Schools Social Competency Program at Wellesley College's Stone Center uses a format known as the Open Circle to teach students all of the essential skills. The program includes training and support for teachers as well as grade-appropriate lesson plans for conducting open circles twice a week. For more information contact Wellesley College, Reach Out to Schools—Social Competency Program, The Stone Center, 106 Central Street, Wellesley, MA 02181-8268, telephone 617-283-2847.

Appendix I

THE CRUCIAL Cs

CONNECT
I need to believe I have a place. I Belong.

CAPABLE
I need to believe I can do it.

COUNT
I need to believe I can make a difference.

COURAGE
I need to believe I can handle what comes.

WHEN WE FEEL CONNECTION WE	WHEN WE DON'T FEEL CONNECTION WE
FEEL: **secure**	FEEL: **insecure,** isolated
DO: Reach out Make friends **Cooperate**	DO: Susceptible to peer pressure May try to get **attention** in negative ways

NEED: Communication Skills

WHEN WE FEEL CAPABLE WE:	WHEN WE DON'T FEEL CAPABLE WE:
FEEL: **competent**	FEEL: **inadequate**
DO: Exhibit self-control Develop **self-reliance**	DO: Try to control others and/ or become defiant May become dependent Seek **power**

NEED: Develop self-discipline

WHEN WE BELIEVE WE COUNT WE:	WHEN WE DON'T BELIEVE WE COUNT WE:
FEEL: **valuable**	FEEL: **insignificant**, hurt
DO: **Contribute**	DO: May try to hurt back or show own pain Seek **revenge**

NEED: Assume responsibility

WHEN WE HAVE COURAGE WE:	WHEN WE DON'T HAVE COURAGE WE:
FEEL: **equal, confident, hopeful**	FEEL: **inferior, defeated, hopeless**
DO: Face challenges, Willing to try Develop **resiliency**	DO: Give up Use **avoidance**

NEED: Good Judgment

Appendix II

The Crucial Cs and Rudolf Dreikurs' Short-Range Goals of Misbehavior

Amy Lew and Betty Lou Bettner

Child's belief	**Child feels**	**Child's negative goal**	**Adult feels**	**Adult's impulse**	**Child's response to correction**
I only count when I'm being noticed.	insecure alienated	**ATTENTION**	irritated annoyed	**REMIND** What, again?	"temporarily" stops
My strength is in showing you that you can't make me and you can't stop me.	inadequate dependent others are in control	**POWER**	angry challenged	**FIGHT** I insist that you do as I say.	misbehavior intensifies
I knew you were against me. No one really likes me. I'll show you how it feels.	insignificant	**REVENGE** get back get even	hurt or wants to punish	**PUNISH** How could you do this to me? us? them? I'll teach you a lesson.	wants to get even makes self disliked
I can't do anything right so I won't try. If I don't try, my failures won't be so obvious.	inferior useless hopeless	**AVOIDANCE** display of inadequacy	despair I give up. hopeless	**GIVE UP** It's no use.	passive no change more hopeless displays inadequacy

Remember: Misbehavior is a symptom of the child's discouragement at not having the Crucial Cs. Use encouragement and training through natural and logical consequences. Consider and agree on choices together.

Crucial Cs	**Constructive Alternatives**	**Child's belief**	**Child feels**	**Child's positive goal**
CONNECT	Replace negative attention with positive attention. Plan activities together. Don't ignore the child; ignore the misbehavior. Teach self-sufficiency.	I belong.	secure	**COOPER-ATION**
CAPABLE	Don't try to win. Give opportunity and choices so child can display power constructively. Maintain friendly attitude.	I can do it.	competent self-control	**SELF-RELIANCE**
COUNT	Avoid anger and hurt feelings. Maintain appreciation in relationship. Offer chances to help. Seek support and help in identifying positives. (Don't give up.)	I matter. I can make a difference.	significant valuable	**CONTRIBU-TION**
COURAGE	Notice only strengths and ignore the negative. Set up steady exposure to manageable tasks that have a guarantee of success. No criticism.	I can handle what comes.	hopeful willing to try	**RESILIENCY**

Appendix III

Teacher Questionnaire

Remember a classroom where you felt really good. What happened in that classroom? How did you feel? What did you do?

Remember a classroom you hated. What happened in that classroom? How did you feel? What did you do?

Remember an experience you had with a teacher that left you feeling positive. What was she or he like? What did that teacher do? How did you feel? What did you do?

Remember a negative experience you had with a teacher. What happened? How did you feel? What did you do?

Please list some things that are happening in your school that increase your feelings of the Crucial Cs (connect, capable, count, courage).

Please list some things that interfere with your feeling the Crucial Cs.

Imagine for a moment that you are asked to leave your classroom and your students are asked to describe you. What words do you hope they would use? What words do you think they would use? What images do you think are important to project as a teacher?

Appendix IV

Recommended Reading

Albert, Linda. *Cooperative Discipline: Revised Edition.* Shoreview, MN: Pearson, 1996.

Bettner, Betty Lou, Editor. *An Adlerian Resource Book: A Sampler of Reproducible Education Materials.* Hershey, PA: North American Society of Adlerian Psychology, 1989 Tel. 312/629-8801.

Bettner, Betty Lou and Lew, Amy. *Raising Kids Who Can: Become Responsible, Self-Reliant, Resilient, Contributing Adults and How to Use Family Meetings to Make It Happen.* Newton Centre, MA: Connexions Press, 2005.

Brooks, Robert. *The Self-Esteem Teacher* Circle Pines, MN: AGS, American Guidance Service, 1991.

Dreikurs, Rudolf. *Psychology in the Classroom,* (Revised). New York: Harper and Row, 1957.

______, Bronia Grunwald and Floy Pepper. *Maintaining Sanity in the Classroom.* New York: Harper and Row, 1982.

______, and Vicki Soltz, *Children: The Challenge.* New York: Hawthorn Books Inc., 1964.

Dweck, Carol S. *Mindset: The New Psychology of Success.* New York: Random House, 2006.

Glenn, H. Stephen and Jane Nelsen, *Raising Self-Reliant Children in a Self-Indulgent World.* Rocklin, CA: Prima Publishing, 1988.

Lott, Lynn and Riki Intner. *The Family That Works Together.* Rocklin, CA: Prima Publishing, 1994.

Nelsen, Jane, H. Stephen Glenn. *Time Out.* Fair Oaks, CA: Sunrise Press. 1991.

______, Lynn Lott and H. Stephen Glenn. *Positive Discipline in the Classroom: How to Effectively Use Class Meetings.* Rocklin, CA: Prima Publishing, 1993.

Main, Frank. *Perfect Parenting and Other Myths.* Minneapolis, MN: CompCare Pub, 1986.

Popkin, Michael. *ActiveTeaching.* Atlanta, GA: Active Parenting Publishers, 1994.

Appendix V

About the Authors

Betty Lou Bettner, PhD, LPC, is in private practice in individual, couple, and family counseling in Media, Pennsylvania. She is an adjunct faculty member of Holy Family University's graduate school in Philadelphia, PA. Betty Lou is a member and former chair of the Advisory Committee of Children and Youth Services of Delaware County. She was a member of the Delegate Assembly of the North American Society of Adlerian Psychology for ten years and served on the Executive Committee. Betty Lou is on the staff of the International Committee of Adlerian Summer Schools and Institutes.

Amy Lew, PhD, LMHC, LMFT, is a clinical mental health counselor in private practice in couple, individual, and family counseling in Newton and Gloucester, Massachusetts. She is on the faculty of the Family Institute of Cambridge. Amy served as a consultant to the Social Competency Program at the Stone Center at Wellesley College. She has served two terms as the vice president of the North American Society of Adlerian Psychology. Amy began her career as an early childhood educator. She is on the editorial board of the International Journal of Marriage and Family Counseling.

In addition to this book, Amy Lew and Betty Lou Bettner have co-authored a similar book for parents entitled *A Parent's Guide to Understanding and Motivating Children*, and a book about family meetings; *Raising Kids Who Can: Become Responsible, Self-Reliant, Resilient, Contributing Adults and How to Use Family Meetings to Make It Happen.* Connexions Press,2005. (The book has been translated into German, Czech, and Estonian.). They have also written a guide for people interested in conducting study groups for parents using the Raising Kids Who Can model*; Raising Kids Who Can Series: A Parent Study Group Leader's Guide***.** They have also written a book, *Cinderella, The Sequel*: *When The Fairy Tale Ends and Real Life Begins*, which uses a lighthearted approach to shed light on some of the common problems that couples confront and offer suggestions for resolving them. Amy and Betty Lou are also the family interventions column editors for the Journal of Individual Psychology.

Appendix VI

Other Books by Amy Lew and Betty Lou Bettner

Raising Kids Who Can

"Easy-to-read, logically presented, and filled with many helpful examples. *Raising Kids Who Can* will not only lead to better family meetings, but to better families." —Michael H. Popkin, author of *Active Parenting.*

"This book is a little gem that succeeds in a big way. *Raising Kids Who Can* lays out a readable, doable map for families (and teachers) seeking to develop structure and cooperation in a friendly atmosphere."—*The Family Psychologist*, American Psychological Association.

"Betty Lou Bettner and Amy Lew have created a fresh, insightful synthesis of strategies for becoming a more functional, responsible, and capable family...This is a book about family meetings, but it is also a book about the bigger picture that makes family meetings (and families) work...The book has a practical approach with a clear writing style."—Don Dinkmeyer, Jr., Ph.D., co-author of *The New STEP* (Systematic Training for Effective Parenting), *STEP/Teen,* and *Early Childhood STEP.*

Raising Kids Who Can has been translated into German, Czech, and Estonian.

A Parent's Guide to Understanding and Motivating Children

"This is a clear and concise guide for all parents. In a very practical way it helps the parents understand their child's behavior and misbehavior. It is a very encouraging book. It is a great relief for someone to put into words the worries we all have as parents and to illustrate techniques that will help in the solution of everyday problems. It deals especially well with creating cooperation within families. I believe it could become your constant companion in the struggle that we all have in trying to bring up our children to be responsible, caring, and likable adults. Highly recommended."—Ruth Farrell, Parents' Network of Ireland.

Raising Kids Who Can Series—Parent Study Group Leader's Guide

This Guide is designed to help parent study group leaders, counselors, social workers and therapists teach the concepts and strategies outlined in *Raising Kids Who Can* and *A Parent's Guide to Understanding and Motivating Children.*

The Leader's Guide is divided into three sections. The first section provides some tips to help you run your groups. The second and third sections present two courses of six sessions each. Both courses emphasize the importance of developing the Crucial Cs, the beliefs that one is **connected** to others, a part of family and community, **capable** of taking care of oneself; and is valued by others, has the knowledge that one **counts** and makes a difference, and has the **courage** needed to meet life's challenges. The courses also focus on how parents can develop four sets of essential skills in their children: **communication** skills, the ability to use **good judgment** and make wise decisions, **self-discipline,** and the ability to **assume responsibility.**

The design of both courses includes brief presentations of relevant material by the Leader, experiential exercises to reinforce the concepts, time to practice new skills, and the opportunity for parents to get help with their concerns.

CINDERELLA, THE SEQUEL (a fairy tale for adults!)

"When the fairy tale ends and real life begins' is the subtitle of this enchanting and therapeutic tale. Lew and Bettner astutely realize that falling in the love and getting married are only the first 'comparatively easy' steps in the process of building a lasting relationship. In *Cinderella, the Sequel* we see what happened between Cinderella and Prince Charming as they learned to live together and understand one another…Lew and Bettner make very helpful concrete suggestions appropriate for any couple who need help continuing to work on a relationship…This charming metaphor would be invaluable to…couples and individuals who struggle with relationships…"—Terry Kottman, Ph.D. (author of Adlerian Play Therapy), The Family Journal, International Association of Marriage and Family Counselors.

Ordering Information

Contact Connexions Press at:

10 Langley Rd Suite 200
Newton Centre, MA 02459
tel.: 617/332-3220
fax: 617/332-7863
e-mail: connexpr@thecia.net
website: www.connexionspress.com

1 Old State Rd
Media, PA 19063
tel.: 610/566-1004
fax: 610/566-1004
e-mail: blbettner@aol.com

Quantity discounts available

****

For information about leader training or in-services and workshops for parents and teachers, please contact Amy Lew and Betty Lou Bettner through Connexions Press.